Lucy's Favorite
Elephant
Jokes

Compiled and edited by
Rob Huberman

COMTEQ™
PUBLISHING
MARGATE, NEW JERSEY

Published by:
    ComteQ Publishing
    A division of ComteQ Communications, LLC
    101 N. Washington Ave. • Suite 2B
    Margate, New Jersey 08402
    609-487-9000 • Fax 609-487-9099
    Email: publisher@ComteQpublishing.com
    Website: www.ComteQpublishing.com

ISBN 978-1-935232-24-7

Cover & book design by Rob Huberman

Printed in the United States of America
10 9 8 7 6 5 4 3 2 1

Contents

What's in that Trunk?

Q: What do an elephant and a car have in common?
A: They both have trunks!

Q: Why do elephants have trunks?
A: They can't afford suitcases!

Q: Why else do elephants have trunks?
A1: Because they'd look silly with glove compartments!

A2: Because they don't have pockets!

Q: If an elephant didn't have a
   trunk, how would he smell?
A: Trunk or no trunk, he'd still smell
   terrible!

Q: What has 6 legs, 3 ears, 4 tusks,
   and 2 trunks?
A: An elephant with spare parts!

Q: Why were the elephants kicked
   out of the swimming pool?
A: They couldn't keep their trunks up!

Q: Why wasn't the elephant allowed on the airplane?
A: Because his trunk wouldn't fit under the seat!

Q: Why were the elephants the last animals off the Noah's ark?
A: Because they had to pack their trunks!

Q: How do you know if an elephant is sleeping over?
A: He will have his pajamas in his trunk!

Q: Why was the elephant angry at the bellboy?
A: He didn't carry his trunk up to his room!

Q: What did the hotel manager say to the
   elephant that couldn't pay his bill?
A: Pack your trunk and clear out!

Q: How does an elephant commit suicide?
A: It sticks its trunk up its butt!

Q: How do you run over an elephant?
A: Climb up his tail, dash to his head, then slide down the trunk!

Q: Why also do elephants have short tails?
A: So they won't get them caught in subway train doors!

Q: Why do elephants have long toenails?
A: To pick their trunks!

Q: Why do elephants have long toenails on Friday?
A: Because their manicurist doesn't come until Saturday!

Q: Why do elephants go to bed late?
A: They spend hours setting their tails!

Q: Why does an elephant have a short
   tail?
A: Someone pulled on his
   trunk!

It's about time!

Q: What time is it when ten
   elephants are chasing you?
A: Ten after one!

Q: If you see an elephant in your car,
   what time is it?
A: Time to get a new car!

Q: What time is it when an elephant sit on your sofa?
A: Time to get a new sofa!

Q: What time is it when an elephant sits on your toilet?
A: Time to run away!

Hey baby!

Q: What do elephants have that nothing else has?
A: Baby elephants.

Q: Where do baby elephants
   come from?
A: Big storks!

Q: What is a baby elephant after
   he is five weeks old?
A: Six weeks old!

Q: How do you raise a baby elephant?
A: With a fork lift truck!

Found a peanut!

Q: What did the peanut say to the elephant?
A: Nothing, peanuts can't talk!

Q: How do you know if an elephant's
   been sleeping in your bed? ?
A: Peanut shells under the pillow!

Q: What did the elephant say when a boy
   brought him broccoli instead of peanuts?
A: Oh, nuts!

Q: How do you know peanuts are fattening?
A: Because you never see a skinny elephant!

Q: How do you know if an elephant is standing next
   to you in an elevator?
A: By the smell of peanuts on their breath!

Q: Why do elephants prefer peanuts to caviar?
A: Because they're easier to get at the ballpark!

Q: Why did the elephant quit working for the circus?
A: He was tired of working for peanuts!

Q: How do you hunt for elephants?
A: Hide in a bush and make a noise like a peanut!

Q: Why do elephants have squinting eyes?
A: From reading the small print on peanut packages!

Q: Why do elephants like peanuts so much?
A: Because they can save the peanut wrappers for valuable prizes!

Don't miss that call!

Q: What do you call two elephants on a bicycle?
A: Optimistic!

Q: What do you call an elephant wearing pink earmuffs and a dress?
A: Anything you want. It can't hear you!

Q: What do you call an elephant in a telephone booth?
A: Stuck!

Q: What do you call an elephant
   that takes a bite out of the
   computer?
A: A mega-byte!

Q: What do you call elephants
   that ride on trains?
A: Passengers!

Q: What do you call an elephant
   at the North Pole?
A: Lost!

Q: What do you call an elephant that lies across the middle
   of a tennis court?
A: Annette!

Q: What do you call an elephant creeping through the jungle in the
   middle of the night?
A: Russell!

Q: What do you call someone with an elephant on their head?
A: Squashed!

Q: What can an elephant with a machine gun call you?
A: Anything he likes!

Q: What do you call an elephant who can't spell his own name?
A: Dumbo!

Q: What do you call an elephant that flies?
A: A jumbo jet!

On the road again!

Q: Why did the elephant cross the road?
A: It was the chicken's day off!

Q: Why did the elephant cross the road?
A: To squash the chicken on the other side!

Q: Why did the elephant cross the road?
A: Because the chicken retired!

Q: Why did the elephant cross the road?
A: To pick up the squashed chicken!

Q: Why did the Frenchman sprinkle salt on the road?
A: To keep elephants away!
   But there are no elephants in France...
   See, it's working!

Q: Why did the elephant lie down in the middle of the road?
A: To trip the ants!

Q: Why did the elephant cross the road?
A: Because the chicken was carrying a peanut!

Q: Why *didn't* the elephant cross the road?
A: He didn't want to be mistaken for a chicken!

How in the world...

Q: How do you smuggle an elephant over the border?
A: Put a slice of bread over each ear and call him your lunch!

Q: How many elephants will fit into a taxi?
A: Four: Two in the front, two in the back!

Q: How many giraffes will fit into a taxi?
A: None. It's full of elephants!

Q: How do you know there are four elephants in your refrigerator?
A: There's an empty taxi parked outside!

Q: How many elephants does it take to change a light bulb?
A: Don't be stupid. Elephants can't change light bulbs!

Q: How do you know if there's an elephant in your bed?
A: He has a big 'E' on his pajamas!

Q: How do you know if there is an elephant under the bed?
A: Your nose is touching the ceiling!

Q: How can you stop an elephant from charging?
A: Take away his credit card!

Q: How else can you stop an elephant from charging?
A: By removing his batteries!

Q: How do you get an elephant into a matchbox?
A: Take out all the matches first!

Q: How do you get an elephant out of the water?
A: Wet!

Q: How do you get two elephants out of the water?
A: One by one!

Q: How can you tell if an elephant is sleeping?
A: When he is in bed with the covers pulled up and wearing pajamas and his pink tennis shoes are off, the chances are he's asleep—if he's snoring! But, watch out, just in case!

Q: How do you housebreak an elephant?
A: You get 14 copies of the New York Times Sunday Edition!

Q: How many elephants can you fit into a Mercedes?
A: Five: two in the front, two in the back and one in the glove compartment!

Q: How many legs does an elephant have?
A: Four, one on each side!

Q: How do you know if you pass an elephant?
A: You can't get the toilet seat down!

Q: How do you make an elephant fly?
A: Start with a three foot zipper!

Q: How do you stop an elephant from passing through
   the eye of a needle?
A: Tie a knot in its tail!

Q: How do elephants dive into swimming pools?
A: Head first!

Q: How do you hire an elephant?
A: Stand it on four bricks!

Q: How to you keep an elephant in suspense?
A: I'll tell you tomorrow!

Q: How does an elephant stuck in a
   tree get down?
A: He doesn't! Even elephants
   know you get down from
   a goose!

Q: But what if you really need
   to get him down?
A: Ask the birds to push him out!

Q: Why do elephants have flat feet?
A: From jumping out of trees!

Q: Why, also, do elephants have flat feet?
A: They don't have arches in their sneakers!

Q: How do you make a slow elephant fast?
A: Don't feed him!

Q: How do you make a statue of an elephant?
A: Get a large rock and carve away all the pieces that don't look like an elephant!

Q: How do you make an elephant stew to serve 1000 guests?
A: Get a gigantic-sized elephant and cook with potatoes, vegetable, and spices. This is enough to serve 500 people. Throw in two rabbits. Now there's enough to serve 1000 people!

Q: How do you catch an elephant?
A: Wait at a street corner and when you see the elephant, raise your hand and yell, "Yo, elephant!"

Q: How does an astronomer catch an elephant?
A: With a telescope, a matchbox and a pair of tweezers. He goes to the jungle and when he sees an elephant, he turns the telescope the wrong way around and looks through it. The elephant is now so small that he can pick it up with the tweezers and put it into the matchbox!

Who, What, When, Where, Why?

Q: What game do elephants like to play most?
A: Squash!

Q: What did the grape say to the elephant?
A: Nothing, grapes can't talk!

Q: Why don't elephants ride bikes?
A: They don't have a thumb to ring the bell!

Q: Why is an elephant big, grey and wrinkly?
A: Because if it was small, white and hard it would be an aspirin!

Q: Why are golf balls small and white?
A: Because if they were big and grey they would be elephants!

Q: What do you get if you take an elephant into the city?
A: Free Parking!

Q: What do you get if you take an elephant into work?
A: Sole use of the elevator!

Q: What do you give a seasick elephant?
A: Lots of room!

Q: How many elephants does it take to screw in a light bulb?
A: Two, but you need a real big bulb!

Q: What is more difficult than getting an elephant into the back seat of your car?
A: Getting TWO elephants into the back seat of your car!

Q: What happens when an elephant sits in front of you at the movies?
A: You miss most of the picture!

Q: Why didn't the elephant like to play cards in the jungle?
A: Because there were too many cheetahs!

Q: What's convenient and weighs 24,000 pounds?
A: An elephant six-pack!

Q: Why do elephants have cracks between their toes?
A: For carrying their library cards!

Q: What's the difference between an elephant and a piece of paper?
A: You can't make a paper airplane out of an elephant!

Q: Why do elephants have gray skin?
A: To hold their insides together!

Q: Why are elephants so wrinkled?
A: Have you ever tried to iron one?

Q: Where do you find elephants?
A: It depends on where you left them!

Q: What do you say when an elephant
   sneezes?
A: *Gesundheit!*

Q: What do you do when an elephant
   sneezes?
A: Get out of the way!

Q: What goes, Clomp, clomp, clomp,
   squish, clomp, clomp, clomp, squish?
A: An elephant with a wet sneaker!

Q: What kind of elephants live at the
   North Pole?
A: Cold ones!

Q: What's as big as an elephant, but doesn't weigh anything?
A: An elephant's shadow!

Q: What was the elephant doing on the freeway?
A: About 5 miles per hour!

Q: Why did the elephant float on its back?
A: So the seagulls could have a naval base!

Q: What is the difference between an elephant and a blueberries?
A: They're both blue, except for the elephant!

Q: What do elephants use for slippers?
A: Sheep!

Q: Why don't elephants pick their noses?
A: Because they don't know what to do with a 20 pound booger!

Q: What did the bunch of grapes say when the elephant
   stepped on them?
A: Nothing, they just let out a little wine!

Q: What did the elephant do when he broke his toe and
   couldn't walk?
A: He called a tow (toe) truck!

Q: What do you do if you get eaten by an elephant?
A: Run around and around inside him until you are all pooped out!

Q: Why do elephants lie on their backs in the
   jungle with
   their feet in the air?
A: To trip birds!

Q: Why does an elephant take a shower?
A: Because he can't fit into the bathtub!

Q: Why do girl elephants wear angora
   sweaters?
A: So you can tell them from boy elephants!

Q: Why don't elephants like blue lace petticoats?
A: Who said they don't like blue lace petticoats?

Q: What did the elephant say when he got caught
   in the revolving door?
A: If this place wants to do much business with elephants,
   they better get bigger revolving doors!

13

Q: What did the nearsighted elephant say when the Volkswagen ran into it?
A: How many times have I told you kids—don't play in the street!

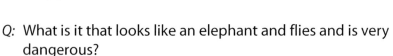

Q: What is it that looks like an elephant and flies?
A: A flying elephant!

Q: Why do elephants walk on four feet?
A: Because if they flew, you could never keep your car clean!

Q: What is it that looks like an elephant and flies and is very dangerous?
A: A flying elephant with a machine gun!

Q: Why don't elephants ride buses during rush hour?
A: They're afraid of pick pockets!

Q: What does an elephant smell like after it takes a shower?
A: A wet elephant!

Q: Which elephants don't get toothaches?
A: Those that brush with Crest!

Q: Why does an elephant never forget?
A: What's he got to remember? Does an elephant have to remember where he parked his car, or his wedding anniversary, or if he left the water running in the sink?

Q: Why do elephants travel in herds?
A: Because if they traveled in flocks, it would confuse the sheepdogs!

Q: What's gray and goes round and round?
A: An elephant in a washing machine!

Q: Why do the elephants have short tails?
A: Because they can't remember long stories!

Q: What's the difference between an injured elephant and bad weather?
A: One roars with pain and the other pours with rain!

Q: What's gray and wrinkly and jumps every twenty seconds?
A: An elephant with hiccups!

Q: What's big and gray and has 16 wheels?
A: An elephant on roller skates!

Q: What goes up slowly and comes down quickly?
A: An elephant in an elevator!

Q: Why does an elephant wear sneakers?
A: So that he can sneak up on mice!

Q: What's the difference between a sick elephant and seven days?
A: One is a weak one and the other one week!

Q: What's the difference between an elephant and a bad student?
A: One rarely bites and the other barely writes!

Q: What did the elephant say when the man grabbed him by the tail?
A: This is the end of me!

Q: What is the easy way to get a wild elephant?
A: Get a tame one and annoy it!

Q: Who lost a herd of elephants?
A: Big Bo Peep!

Q: What can you do with old cannon balls?
A: Give them to elephants to use as marbles!

Q: Why do elephants have wrinkled knees?
A: From playing marbles!

Q: Why do elephants have dirty knees?
A: From praying for rain!

Q: Why do elephants drink so much?
A: To try to forget!

Q: Why can't elephants hitchhike?
A: They don't have thumbs!

Q: How do you know if you pass an elephant?
A: You can't get the toilet seat down!

Q: Why do elephants squirt water through their noses?
A: If they squirted it through their tails, it'd be very difficult to aim!

Q: What is the pink stuff between an elephant's toes?
A: Slow circus clowns!

Q: Which side of an elephant has the most skin?
A: The outside!

Q: Why do elephants wear glasses?
A: To make sure they don't step on other elephants!

Q: What do you give an elephant with big feet?
A: Plenty of room!

Q: What's the difference between a biscuit and an elephant?
A: You can't dip an elephant into your tea!

Q: Why did the big game hunter give up hunting elephants?
A: He got tired of carrying the decoys!

Q: What steps would you take if you were being chased by an elephant?
A: Big ones!

Q: Why do elephants have toenails?
A: So they can have something to chew on when they're nervous!

Q: Why do elephants have sore ankles?
A: From wearing their sneakers too tight!

Q: Can an elephant jump higher than a lamppost?
A: Yes. A lamppost can't jump at all!

Q: Why do elephants wear sneakers while jumping from tree to tree?
A: They don't want to wake up the neighbors!

Q: Why do elephants climb up palm trees?
A: To try out their new sneakers!

Q: What's the difference between a girl elephant and a boy elephant?
A: One sings soprano, one sings bass!

Q: Why do elephants wear short-shorts?
A: You'd sweat too, if you wore long pants in the jungle heat!

Q: Why do elephants catch colds?
A: You would too if you ran around without any clothes on!

Q: How can you tell if there's an elephant on your back during a hurricane?
A: You'll hear his ears flapping in the wind!

Q: Why do elephants float down the river on their backs?
A: They don't want to get their tennis shoes wet!

Q: Why do elephants wear tennies?
A: Because ninies are too small!

Q: Why don't elephants listen to the radio?
A: They don't have fingers to turn the dial!

Q: Why don't elephants take ballet lessons?
A: They've outgrown their leotards!

Q: Why do elephants never lie!
A: The jungle floor isn't very comfortable!

Q: Where do you find elephants?
A: It depends on where you leave them!

Q: Why do elephants have white tusks?
A: They use the Crest whitening strips!

Q: Why do elephants' tusks stick way out?
A: Because their parents won't allow them to get braces!

Q: Where also do you find elephants?
A: Elephants are so darned big that they hardly ever get lost!

Q: Why do elephants roll down the hill?
A: Because they can't roll up very well!

Q: Why don't many elephants go to college?
A: Because they don't finish high school!

Q: What color hair tint do elephants use?
A: How would I know? Only their hairdressers know for sure!

Q: What sound you get when you drop an elephant down a mineshaft?
A: A-flat minor!

Q: What sound do you get when you drop an elephant into an army camp?
A: A-flat major!

Q: What would you get if Batman & Robin were run over by a herd of elephants?
A: Flatman and Ribbon!

Q: Why did the elephant lie on his back in the water and stick his feet up?
A: So you could tell him from a bar of Ivory soap!

Q: What do elephants do for laughs?
A: They tell people jokes!

Q: Why did the elephant and the donkey fight?
A: It was an election year!

Q: How do you get an elephant on top of an oak tree?
A: Stand him on an acorn and wait fifty years!

Q: What if you don't want to wait fifty years?
A: Parachute him from an airplane!

Q: Why isn't it safe to climb oak trees between 1:00 and 2:00 in the afternoon?
A: Because that is when the elephants practice their parachute jumping!

Q: Why do elephants have round, flat feet?
A: To help them walk on the lily pads in the ponds!

Q: Why do elephants walk on the lily pads?
A: To keep them from sinking into the water!

Q: Why isn't it safe to go onto the ponds between 3:00 and 4:00 in the afternoon?
A: That's when the elephants are walking on the lily pads!

Q: Why are frogs such good jumpers?
A: They like to sit on the lily pads between 3:00 and 4:00 in the afternoon!

Elephants & Animals

Q: What is gray, has four legs and a trunk?
A: A mouse going to the beach on vacation!

Q: What is tan, has four legs and a trunk?
A: A mouse coming back from vacation!

Q: What has eight legs, two trunks, four eyes and two tails?
A: Two elephants!

Q: How do you get down off an elephant?
A: You don't. You get down off of a goose!

Q: What did the cat say to the elephant?
A: Meow!

Q: What's the difference between an African elephant
   and an Indian elephant?
A: About 3000 miles!

Q: What's the difference between an elephant and a flea?
A: An elephant can have fleas, but a flea can't have elephants!

Q: What's the difference between a
   chicken and an elephant?
A: An elephant can have chicken pox
   but a chicken cannot have elephant
   pox!

Q: What's the difference between an
   elephant and an egg?
A: If you don't know, I hope you don't do
   the grocery shopping!

Q: Why do elephants wear sandals?
A: So that they don't sink into the sand!

Q: Why do ostriches stick their head into the ground?
A: To look for the elephants who forgot to wear their sandals!

Q: Why do ducks have flat feet?
A: From stamping out forest fires!

Q: Why do elephants have flat feet?
A: From stamping out flaming ducks!

Q: Why do giraffes have long necks
A: For spitting on burning elephants!

Q: Why did the elf marry the ant?
A: He wanted to have elf-ants!

Q: What do you get if you cross an
   elephant with a kangaroo?
A: Big holes all over Australia!

Q: What do you get if you cross two fish with two elephants?
A: A pair of swimming trunks!

Q: What do you get if you cross an elephant with a flea or tick?
A: A very worried dog!

Q: What do you get if you cross an elephant with a whale?
A: A submarine with a built-in snorkel!

Q: What do you get when you cross an elephant with a hamster?
A: A smashed hamster!

Q: What to you get if you cross a parrot with an elephant?
A: An animal that tells you everything that it remembers!

Q: How to you tell the difference between an elephant and a mouse?
A: Try picking them up!

Q: How are an elephant and a hippopotamus alike?
A: Neither can play basketball!

Q: What is stronger, an elephant or a snail?
A: A snail, because it carries its whole house— an elephant just carries its trunk!

Q: Why don't elephants eat penguins?
A: Because they can't get the wrappers off!

Q: Why is an elephant big, grey and wrinkled?
A: Because if it were small, fluffy and yellow it would be a canary!

Q: What do you get if you cross an elephant with a canary?
A: A very messy birdcage!

Q: What do you get when you cross an elephant with a wad of gum?
A: An elephant that sticks to the bottom of your shoe or gum that never forgets!

Q: How does an elephant put his trunk into a crocodile's mouth?
A: VERY carefully!

Q: What does a bald elephant wear for a toupee?
A: A sheep!

Q: Why is an elephant braver than a hen?
A: Because the elephant isn't a chicken!

Q: What is worse than raining cats
   and dogs?
A: Raining elephants!

Q: Which takes less time to prepare
   for a trip, a rooster or an elephant?
A: A rooster…he only takes his comb!

Q: When you buy elephants, what
   should you always check for first?
A: The Good Housekeeping
   "Seal" of Approval!

Q: What do you do with an elephant with three balls?
A: Walk him and pitch to the giraffe!

Q: What's worse than an elephant on water skis?
A: A porcupine on a rubber life raft!

Elephants by Color

Q: What should you do to a blue elephant?
A: Cheer it up!

Q: What should you do to a green elephant?
A: Wait until it gets ripe!

Q: What should you do to a yellow elephant?
A: Try to teach it to be brave!

Q: What should you do to a white elephant?
A: Hold its nose until it turns blue, then follow the directions for a blue elephant!

Q: What is large and gray and goes around and around in circles?
A: An elephant stuck in a revolving door!

Q: Why do elephants wear shoes with yellow soles?
A: So you don't see them when they float upside down in a bowl of custard!

Q: Have you ever seen an elephant floating upside down in a bowl of custard?
A: No, of course not. That camouflage is still working!

Q: Why do elephants wear red toenail polish?
A: Oops, sorry, no Polish jokes allowed in this book!

Q: Why do elephants paint their toenails red?
A: So they can hide in the strawberry patch.
    But there aren't any elephants in the strawberry patch!
    See, their camouflage is working!

Q: Why do elephants hide in strawberry patches?
A: So they can jump out and stomp on people!

Q: Why do elephants live in herds?
A: To get a wholesale discount on the shoes with yellow soles!

Q: How do you shoot a blue elephant?
A: With a blue elephant gun, of course!

Q: How do you shoot a red elephant?
A: Hold his trunk shut until he turns blue, and then shoot him with the blue elephant gun!

Q: How do you shoot a yellow elephant?
A: Ever seen a yellow elephant?

Q: Why do elephants wear tiny green hats?
A: To tiptoe across a pool table without being seen!

Q: What do you know when you see three elephants walking down the street wearing pink sweatshirts?
A: They're all on the same team!

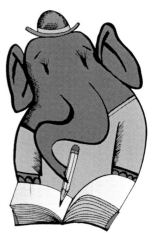

Q: What do you call an elephant wearing pink earmuffs and a dress?
A: Anything you want. It can't hear you!

Q: What's gray and yellow and gray and yellow and gray and yellow?
A: An elephant rolling down a hill with a daisy in its mouth!

Q: What's gray and yellow and gray and yellow and gray and yellow, THUMP, gray and black and blue and black and blue?
A: An elephant rolling down a hill with a daisy in its mouth that hit a rock!

Q: Why did the elephant paint each of her toenails a different color?
A: So she could hide in a bag of M&Ms!

Q: What's grey and white on the inside and red on the outside?
A: An inside-out elephant!

Q: What's yellow on the outside, but gray in the inside?
A: A school bus full of elephants!

Q: What else is yellow on the outside and grey on the inside?
A: An elephant disguised as a banana!

Q: How are an elephant and a banana just alike?
A: They are both yellow, except for the elephant, of course!

Q: What is grey and not there?
A: No elephants!

Q: Why did the elephant have three white shoes and one yellow?
A: 'Cause he forgot to lift his leg!

Q: What is grey and purple and pink and orange and yellow and blue and green and brown and black and white and red?
A: An elephant holding a box of crayons!

Q: Why did the elephant wear pink pajamas?
A: Because his blue ones were in the wash!!

Q: Why are elephants big and gray?
A: Because if they were small and red they would be apples!

Q: Why did the elephant walk around in her polka dotted socks?
A: Somebody stole her yellow sole shoes!

Q: What's grey, stands in a river when it rains and doesn't get wet?
A: An elephant with an umbrella!

Q: What's grey with red spots?
A: An elephant with the measles!

Q: What's big and grey and has horns?
A: An elephant marching band!

Q: Why are elephants trumpeters?
A: Because it's too hard for them to learn the piano!

Q: What's grey, has four legs and jumps up and down?
A: An elephant on a trampoline!

Q: What's grey and wrinkly and jumps every twenty seconds?
A: An elephant with hiccups!

Q: What do you call an elephant that's small and pink?
A: A failure!

Q: What's grey and lights up?
A: An electric elephant!

Q: What's big and grey and mutters?
A: A mumbo Jumbo!

Q: Why did the elephant paint his head yellow?
A: To see if blonds had more fun!

Q: What weighs four tons and is bright red?
A: An elephant holding its breath!

Q: What else weighs four tons and is bright red all over?
A: An embarrassed elephant!

Q: What's else weighs four tons and is bright red all over?
A: A elephant who forgot his suntan lotion!

Q: What's big and green and slimy and
      hangs from trees?
A: Elephant boogers!

Q: Why do elephants wear
      pink tennis shoes?
A: Because white
      ones get dirty too
      fast!

Q: Why do elephants float
      down the river on their
      backs?
A: So they won't get their
      pink tennis shoes wet, silly!

Q: Why do elephants have wrinkled ankles?
A: Because their pink tennis shoes are too
      tight!

Q: Why do elephants wear green tennis
      shoes?
A: To hide in the grass!

Q: Why are elephants grey?
A: So you can tell them from flamingos!

Elephant Food

Q: What's red and white on the outside but gray and white on the inside?
A: Campbell's Cream of Elephant Soup!

Q: How do you make instant elephant?
A: Open the package, add water, and run!

Q: What's the difference between eating an elephant or peanut butter?
A: Elephant doesn't stick to the roof of your mouth!

Q: How do you smuggle an elephant across the border?
A: Put a slice of bread on each side, and call him lunch!

Q: How is an elephant like an apricot?
A: They are both gray. Well, except the apricot!

Q: What's the difference between a dozen eggs and an elephant?
A: If you don't know, I'm sure not going to send you to the store for a dozen eggs!

Q: What the difference between a herd of elephants and a bunch of grapes?
A: Grapes are purple, elephants are gray!

Q: What did the grape say when the elephant stepped on it?
A: Nothing. It just let out a little whine!

Q: Why did the elephant stand on the marshmallow?
A: So he wouldn't fall into the hot chocolate!

Q: Why did the elephant wear red sneakers?
A: So he could hide in the apple tree!

Q: How do you make a hamburger for an elephant?
A: First you take 50 jars of mustard, 60 gallons of ketchup, 10 pounds of onions and then you get this BIG BIG bun....

Q: What do elephants eat besides hamburgers?
A: Canned elephant food!

Q: Why do elephants eat a lot of raw food?
A: Because they don't know how to cook!

Q: Why did the elephant eat the flashlight?
A: He wanted some light refreshment!

Q: Have you heard about the elephant that went on a crash diet?
A: He wrecked three cars, a bus and two trucks!

Q: What's big and grey and loves curry?
A: An Indian elephant!

Q: Why don't elephants like martinis?
A: Did you ever try to get an olive out of your nose?

Q: How do you make an elephant float?
A: With two scoops of ice-cream, a bottle of cream soda, and one elephant!

Q: What did the banana say to the elephant?
A: Nothing. Bananas can't talk, silly!

Q: What's the difference between an elephant and a banana?
A: Have you ever tried to peel an elephant?

Q: How can you tell if there is an elephant in your dessert?
A: You get very lumpy ice cream!

Q: Why are elephants wiser than chickens?
A: Have you ever heard of Kentucky
   Fried Elephant?!

Q: What do you get when you cross
   and elephant with a chicken?
A: I don't know, but Colonel Sanders
   would have fun trying to dip it in
   the batter, wouldn't he?

Q: How do you get an elephant out of
   a box of Jello?
A: Follow the directions on the back
   of the package!

Q: How do you make an elephant sandwich?
A: First of all, you get a very large loaf...

Q: How do you make an elephant stew?
A: Keep him waiting for a few hours!

Q: What do you get when you cross an elephant with peanut butter?
A: Either an elephants that spreads easily;
   or an elephant that sticks to the roof of your mouth;
   or peanut butter that never forgets!

Elephants in the Fridge

Q: How can you tell when an elephant has been in your refrigerator?
A: Look for elephant tracks in the butter!

Q: How do you tell if there are two elephants in your refrigerator?
A: Look for two sets of footprints side by side!

Q: How do you get an elephant into a Volkswagon Beetle?
A: Open the door, insert elephant, close door!

Q: How do you get four elephants into a Volkswagon?
A: Two in the front and two in the back!

Q: How do you put an elephant into a refrigerator?
A: Open the Volkswagen door, take the elephant out, close the Volkswagen door, open the refrigerator, put the elephant inside, close the refrigerator door!

Q: How do you know if an elephant is visiting your refrigerator?
A: There is a Volkswagon parked outside with three elephants in it!

Q: How do you tell if there are three elephants in your refrigerator?
A: The door won't close and there's a Volkswagon parked outside with one elephant in it!

Q: How do you get eight elephants into a refrigerator?
A: Put four elephants into one Volkswagon, put four elephants into another Volkswagon, and put the two Volkswagons into the refrigerator!

Q: But will two Volkswagons fit into a refrigerator?
A: Well, you just took two elephants out of there— and a Volkswagon isn't even as big as an elephant!

Q: How do you get a giraffe into the refrigerator?
A: Open door; remove elephants; insert giraffe; close door!

Q: The lion, the king of the jungle, decided to have a party. He invited all the animals in the jungle, and they all came except one. Which one?
A: The giraffe, because he was still in the refrigerator!

Punny Elephants

Q: What can you send an elephant
   to cheer it up when it is sick?
A: A Get Wellephant Card!

Q: How do elephants communicate
   long distance?
A: They talk on the elephone!

Q: What is beautiful, gray, weighs
   6000 pounds and wears glass
   slippers?
A: Cinderelephant!

Q: What is big and grey and can fly straight up?
A: An elecopter!

Q: What do elephants do for entertainment?
A: Watch elevision!

Q: What's gray, has large wings, a long nose, and gives
   money to elephants?
A: The Tusk Fairy!

Q: What kind of doctors do elephants with skin problems go to?
A: Pachydermatologists!

Q: What do you get when you cross an elephant with a rhinoceros?
A: Eliphino! (hell-if-I-know!)

Q: What do you call a large, grey animal that rings?
A: A Bellephant!

Q: What's big and gray and lives in a lake in Scotland?
A: The Loch Ness Elephant!

Q: Whom do elephants get their Christmas presents from?
A: Elephanta Claus!

Q: What do elephants sing at Christmas?
A: Noel-ephants, Noel-ephants…

Q: What do you find in elephant graveyards?
A: Elephantoms!

Q: What's big, grey, sings and wears a mask?
A: The Elephantom of the Opera!

Q: What is an elephant's favorite movie?
A: Elephantasia!

Q: What do elephants say as a compliment?
A: You look elephantastic!

Q: What's big and grey and protects you from the rain?
A: An umbrellaphant!

Q: What do you get if you cross an elephant with the abominable snowman?
A: A jumbo yeti!

Q: What pills would you give to an elephant that has trouble sleeping?
A: Trunquilizers!

Q: With what words would you scold a bad elephant?
A: Tusk, tusk!

Q: Where is an elephant's favorite place to vacation?
A: Tuscany!

Q: What's the biggest kind of ant in the world?
A: Eleph-ant!

Q: What do you call an elephant that is only three feet high?
A: Trunkated!

Q: Who is the most famous male singing elephant?
A: Harry Elephante!

Q: Who is the most famous female singing elephant?
A: Elephants Gerald!

Q: Where is the safest place to watch a herd of charging elephants?
A: On elevision!

Q: What's grey and puts out forest fires?
A: Smokey the Elephant!

Q: What's Smokey The Elephant's middle name?
Λ: The!

Q: What do you call a elephant that never washes?
A: A smellyphant!

37

Tarzan and the Elephants

Q: What's the difference between an elephant and a plum?
A: Plums are purple!

Q: What did Tarzan say to Jane when he saw a herd
of elephants coming?
A: Here come the elephants!

Q: What did Jane say to Tarzan when she saw a herd of elephants
coming?
A: Here come the plums! (Jane is color blind.)

Q: What did Tarzan say when he saw a herd of elephants in the
distance?
A: Look, a herd of elephants in the distance!

Q: Why did the elephants wear dark
sunglasses?
A: So they wouldn't be recognized!

Q: What did Tarzan say when he saw a
herd of elephants in the distance
wearing sunglasses?
A: Nothing. He doesn't recognize them!

Q: What did Tarzan say when he saw a
herd of giraffes in the distance
wearing sunglasses?
A: Ha ha you elephants! You fooled me once with those
sunglasses , but not this time!

Q: Why are pygmies so short?
A: They listened to Jane and looked for the plums!

Q: If you are colorblind, then how can you tell an elephant from a grape?
A: Stomp around on it for a while. If you don't get any wine, then it's an elephant!

Q: What did Tarzan say when he saw the male elephant jump off the cliff?
A: That's the way the bull bounces!

Q: How many Tarzans can you put into a refrigerator?
A: One silly…there is only one Tarzan!

Q: How do actually you get Tarzan into the refrigerator?
A: Open door, take the two Volkswagons with the elephants out, put Tarzan in, close the door!

Q: Why are there so many elephants running around in the jungle?
A: Tarzan's refrigerator isn't large enough to hold them all!

Tarzan was really tired when he came home after a long day in the jungle.

"What have you been doing all day?" asked Jane.

"Chasing a herd of elephants on the vines," answered Tarzan.

"Really?" said Jane. "I thought that elephants stayed only on the ground!"

Talking about Elephants...

It was a boring Sunday afternoon in the jungle so the Elephants decided to challenge the Ants to a game of soccer. The game was going well with the Elephants beating the Ants ten goals to none, when the Ants gained possession.

The Ants' star player was dribbling the ball towards the Elephants' goal when the Elephant defender came lumbering towards him to block the shot. Then elephant put his foot on the little Ant, crushing him.

The referee immediately ejected the Elephant from the game, shouting, "What do you think you're doing? Do you call that sportsmanship, crushing another player?"

The elephant apologized, explaining, "Well, I didn't mean to crush him—I was just trying to trip him up!"

Teacher: To which family does the elephant belong?
Student: I don't know. Nobody I know owns one!

Teacher: How do you spell elephant?
Student: E-l-l-i-f-i-n-t
Teacher: That's not how the dictionary spells it.
Student: You didn't ask me how the dictionary spells it!

Teacher: Name six wild animals.
Student: Four elephants and two lions!

Teacher: Where would you find an elephant?
Student: You don't have to find them, they're too big to lose!

Bill: My homework is really difficult tonight, I' have to write an essay on an elephant.
Bert: Well, for a start, your're going to need a big ladder!

Susie: What's the difference between an elephant and a matterbaby?
George: What's a matterbaby?
Susie: Nothing, but thanks for asking!

A man went into a restaurant and sat down. He was looking around when he noticed a sign on the wall that stated, "If you ask for something and we can't serve it to you, we will pay you $100."

The man thought for a while and when the waiter came for his order, he said, "I'd like elephant ears on toast please."

"Wheat or white toast, sir? the waiter asked.

The man smiled, sure that there was no way they could serve him elephant ears on toast. "White toast please."

The man sat and waited. Eventually the waiter came back and handed him $100. The man smiled. "I knew you'd have to pay me the $100 for not having elephant ears," he said.

"Actually sir," replied the waiter, "I'm afraid we've run out of wheat bread!"

Knock Knock
Who's there?
Elephants
Elephants Who?
Ella Fintzgerald!

Elephant Trainer: My elephant's got no trunk.
Zookeeper: How does it smell?
Elephant Trainer: Terrible!

Elephant Trainer: My Elephant isn't well. Do you know a good animal doctor?
Zoo Keeper: No. All the doctors I know are people!

Elephant Trainer: I've lost one of my elephants.
Zookeeper: Why don't you put an ad for him in the newspaper's "lost & found" section?
Elephant Trainer: Don't be silly, my elephant can't read!

Elephant Trainer: Doctor, my elephant swallowed someone's camera with a roll of film in it!
Vet: Don't worry sir. Nothing will develop!

Policeman: One of your elephants has been seen chasing a man on a bicycle.
Zookeeper: Nonsense, none of my elephants knows how to ride a bicycle!

A boy with an elephant on his head went to see a doctor The doctor said, "You know you really need help."

"Yes I do," replied the elephant. "Get this kid off my foot!"

One way to catch elephants:
Hide in the grass and make a noise like a peanut!

A man was sprinkling some white powder on his lawn.

"Why are you doing that?" asked his neighbor.

"It's to keep the elephants off the grass," the man replied.

"But we don't get elephants round here!" exclaimed the neighbor.

"I know -— good stuff isn't it!"

Alex: Why do elephants paint their nails different colors?

Samantha: So they can hide in a bubble gum machine!

Alex: I've never seen an elephant in a bubble gum machine!

Samantha: See, it works!

One day an elephant and an ant were each riding their motorbikes when they got into a head-on collision with each other. The elephant had to be taken to the hospital, but the ant did not even get hurt.

Why? Because he was wearing his helmet!

An elephant was walking through a park, stepping on many tiny ants along the way. Upset, the ants decided to crawl up onto the elephant — first up his legs and then up all over his body.

When the elephant started feeling all the little ants on him, he shook hard, making all the ants fall back to the ground, except for one last ant.

As the only ant on the elephant hung on close to the elephant's neck, the all the ants on the ground shouted, "Strangle him! Strangle him!"

Q: Why did the elephant wear sunglasses?
A: With all the silly elephant jokes going around, it didn't want to be recognized!